CW00386410

SPEAK TRUTH SERIES

BOOK ONE

Personalised bible verses that speak God's truth over your situations

Fran Penberthy

Copyright © 2020 by Fran Penberthy

All rights reserved, including the right of reproduction in
whole or in part in any form. No portion of this book may be
reproduced in any form whatsoever, except for brief quota-
tions in reviews, without the written permission.

ISBN: 9798643799856

Contents

INTRODUCTION

Lamentations 3:19-20 "Just thinking about my troubles and my lonely wandering, makes me miserable. That's all I ever think about and I'm depressed". *Contemporary English Version*

v21-23 "Then I remember something that fills me with hope. The Lord's kindness never fails...The Lord can always be trusted to show mercy each morning". *Contemporary English Version*

One thought brings depression but switching to a different thought brings hope. Can it really be as simple as that?

God's word is power. It's His living word that brings us power and authority in every single situation we ever find ourselves in.

The problem comes when we don't know what it says. We are then left to our own thoughts and more often than not, our emotions take over and dictate how we think and act. When emotions drive our thoughts we are at the mercy of how we feel each day and end up blowing hot and cold at the drop of a hat.

For many years, even as a Christian, I had no idea how to handle my thoughts and emotions. There was a negative tape running in my head all the time, negative thoughts that had been there since childhood. I felt powerless to change them. Actually, worse than that, I believed every single negative thought so saw no hope of ever changing them. After all, they were all true.

I had no idea that I could choose what I thought about.

You see, we never have an empty head, we are thinking all the time and if we don't purposefully choose what we think about then other things will choose for us - our childhoods, our past experiences, hurtful words spoken over us, hateful people, difficult situations, sugar-induced moodiness, caffeine overdoses, hormonal imbalances, exhaustion or lack of sleep, to name just a few.

There's a thousand things that will press in and tell you to think depressing thoughts, hopeless thoughts, victim thoughts, unforgiving thoughts.

It's surprisingly easy to be a Christian who sincerely loves Jesus and genuinely wants to please Him in everything you do, while at the same time finding that your faith and trust in Him go up and down daily, a rollercoaster of highs and lows driven by how you feel when you get out of bed in the morning.

What a turnaround began in my own life when God began to shine His light on my unstable emotions. He challenged me to stop, and take some time to face my emotions. To dig down to the roots of what was driving my feelings of loneliness, shame and guilt.

These root beliefs had been formed during my turbulent and deeply unhappy childhood but I couldn't blame my childhood, at some point I had chosen to believe them and make them my own. In fact more than that, they had become such deep seated beliefs that I couldn't be separated from them, they were who I believed I was.

I had come to believe that I couldn't apply the Word of God to them as that would have stripped me of my personality. Plus of course, I was busy blaming everyone and everything else for my unhappy moods. My prayers were full of, "God I'm so sorry, I'm such a failure, please change everyone else so that I can be a better person".

God directed me to find bible verses that spoke the opposite to the roots. The root 'abandonment' for example, He was telling me to find verses about my security in Him, my place in the family, His promise to never leave me etc.

Next, I had to personalise the verses to stop me from seeing them as verses for everyone else but not for me and then to speak them out loud daily. I learned to speak them out with attitude, as if I really believed them, and over time, I did!

God's word is living and active and is not without effect so I shouldn't have been surprised.

My prayer is that this small book will be the start of your breakthrough too!

I have spent time researching every single verse in this book, comparing different translations, sometimes going back to the Greek or Hebrew for the original meaning and sometimes checking dictionary definitions of particular words.

As a result, I have not put any references to the bible translations I've used. Many of these declarations are made up of a number of translations because I have chosen words and expressions that I felt conveyed the truth contained in the verse, in an easy, down to earth and PERSONAL way.

You see, it's so easy to read the bible with blinkers on. We love His word and believe it to be true... But... Not for my situation. He can't use me. Jesus has set me free but I'm stuck with my addiction/hot temper/depression. On and on go the excuses.

By personalising the verse we cut through those lies and we speak God's truth out loud where we can hear it and over time be transformed by it. Plus, we are declaring truth to principalities and powers who have been used to dropping negatives into our thinking and who now need to be told - no more!

God loves you so much and <u>has</u> given you all the resources of heaven so that you <u>can</u> reign in life.

Begin today to speak out truth and watch the changes that take place in your life as you learn to 'take every thought captive and make it obedient to Christ" 2 Corinthians 10:5.

PRAYER TO FOLLOW JESUS

Dear God I'm so tired of trying to be 'good'. My best efforts go wrong all the time. I don't do the things I should and I'm always doing things that end up hurting other people or that damage me.

I want a relationship with You God and I believe that You sent Your Son Jesus to die in my place for my sins. I believe that I am a sinner and I'm so sorry for all the things that I've done wrong over my life. Not just my actions but my words and my thoughts too. I know that they have too often been hateful, unforgiving or full of my own self-importance.

Please remind me right now of specific thoughts, words or actions that I need to repent of. *(Take a few moments to listen and make a note of anything and everything that pops into your mind).*

(Now say sorry for each separate item on your list and remember that repentance means that we stop doing those things).

Thank You for reminding me of those things. I believe that as I have confessed my sins to You that You have forgiven me. I accept Your forgiveness and I refuse to keep beating myself up for past sins. I receive Your forgiveness and Your cleansing. I was guilty of those things but now You declare me innocent because my sins were paid for by Jesus on the cross. I place my trust completely in You and I believe You have set me free.

I believe that Jesus, You rose from the dead to rescue me and give me eternal life. I will never be condemned by You because You have saved me.

I am now a new creation in Christ, my old life is finished and I have a brand new life in Jesus. Jesus I ask You to rule and reign in my life as my Lord and King and I receive Your Holy Spirit to come and live in me now for He is the guarantee that I have eternal life.

ASSURANCE OF SALVATION

John 3:16-17

Father I believe that You so loved the world that You sent Your only Son Jesus to rescue me and give me eternal life. I will never be condemned by You because You have saved me.

Revelation 3:20

Jesus You are knocking on the door to my heart. I hear Your voice and I choose to open the door to You. I thank You that You promise to come in and make Your home with me.

Romans 6:22

I have been set free and become a servant of God and I have received the benefits; holiness and eternal life.

1 Peter 1:8-9

I haven't seen You Jesus but I love You. I can't see You but I believe in You and I am filled with an indescribable joy and glory as I receive the salvation of my soul.

Colossians 1:21-22

I have been released from acting as if I am alienated from God. The truth is I have been reconciled by Christ's death on a cross and I am now presented holy in His sight.

1 Corinthians 6:17

I am united with Christ and I am one with Him in spirit.

Romans 8:2

Thank You Holy Spirit that You have given me life through Christ Jesus and You have set me free from the law of sin and death.

Ephesians 1:7

Through the blood of Jesus I have been set free from my sins, thank You Father that You have forgiven my offences because of Your overflowing kindness.

Romans 8:15

I refuse to still think like a fearful slave, I have received the Spirit of sonship. I am God's adopted child and I cry out 'papa' to you my loving heavenly Father.

Hebrews 2:14-15

Jesus You became flesh and blood and by Your death You destroyed the devil who had power of death. I am now free of my fear of death that held me in bondage.

Romans 10:9-13

I have spoken out that Jesus is Lord and I believe in my heart that God raised Him from the dead so I am saved. I believe Your word that whoever believes in Jesus will never be put to shame. You have poured out Your riches on me because I called on the name of the Lord to be saved.

Mark 16:16

I believe in Jesus and I have been baptised and so I have received your salvation.

Romans 4:5

I do not rely on my own efforts to be saved, I rely on God who declared me innocent when I was guilty. I place my faith 100% in His righteousness not my own.

John 5:24

I heard the gospel and believed in God the Father who sent Jesus so I now have eternal life. I will never be judged, I have already passed from death to life.

John 10:29

Father You are greater than anything, no one can ever snatch me out of Your hand.

DANCING IN THE STORM

Job 1:20

Even when the worst happens I choose to worship You Lord, may Your Name be praised.

Psalm 86:7

Whenever I have trouble I choose to call out to You in complete confidence that You hear me.

Psalm 102

Even when my heart is blighted and withered as grass, even when I feel thrown aside I will declare Your majesty and power I will declare Your faithfulness and compassion.

Lamentations 2:11+19

When my eyes fail from weeping and I am in torment inside, I will pour out my heart like water in the presence of the Lord. I will lift up my hands to Him for the lives of my children.

Lamentations 3:20-25

When I am overwhelmed by my problems and my soul is downcast within me, I stir myself, I recall what I know about God and I have fresh hope - His great love, His compassion, His faithfulness and His goodness.

1 Peter 5:7-8

I throw off worry and fretfulness, I cast all my anxieties onto You Lord because You care for me.

2 Corinthians 2:14

I will never give up, never accept defeat. God always leads me in triumph.

Matthew 28:20 and Hebrews 13:5

I refuse feelings of loneliness as a lie of the enemy and I declare that Jesus is with me always. He will never leave me or forsake me.

John 16:33

I resist the pressures of life, I lay them onto Jesus to carry them because He has overcome the world and its troubles.

Romans 8:37

I am not a failure, I am a conqueror in all things through Christ.

Habakkuk 3:17-18

When I don't have enough resources and everything's going wrong, in the face of that, I choose to worship You Lord and I cultivate joy because You are the God who saves me.

John 14:27

I have peace in the middle of this storm, the peace that You Jesus have put there. Be still my heart, don't be troubled or afraid because His peace isn't going anywhere.

Psalm 34:18

I feel heartbroken Lord but You have promised that You are near me and You save me when I feel crushed in spirit.

2 Corinthians 1:3-4

I choose right now to worship You Father and I thank You for the saving power of Jesus. Father, You are full of mercy and You are here comforting me right now, I receive it. Your comfort in me is so powerful that I am enabled to be a comfort to others going through the same things as me.

Psalm 94:18-19

My thoughts say that my foot is slipping but You say that Your steadfast love is holding me up. The cares in my heart feel many but Your comfort cheers me up.

FEELING ALONE OR ABANDONED

Psalm 25:1+7,15-16

Father I am feeling lonely and desolate right now but I choose to fix my eyes back on You because You always free my feet from the trap. I place my trust in You afresh and remember that You are always good to me.

Psalm 68:6

Father You have set me in a family.

Psalm 91:4

You Lord cover me with Your feathers and under Your wings I find refuge.

Psalm 91:11

You command Your angels to guard me in all my ways.

Psalm 91:14-15

Father You know I love You. I thank You that You protect me, deliver me and honour me and when I call out to You, You always answer me.

Psalm 42:8

By day You direct Your love on me and by night Your song is with me.

Deuteronomy 4:31

Father You will not abandon or destroy me.

Psalm 16:10

Father You will not abandon me to death.

Deuteronomy 31:6

I am strong and full of courage because Father You are always at my side, You will never leave me or abandon me.

Psalm 27:5

In trouble You keep me safe in Your dwelling, You hide me in the shelter of Your tabernacle.

Psalm 27:10

Though my parents forsake me, You Father receive me.

Zephaniah 3:17

Father You are with me

You are mighty to save

You delight in me

You quiet me with Your love

You rejoice over me with singing

Romans 5:5

I am free of shame and full of hope because You Lord have poured out Your love into my heart by the Holy Spirit.

Romans 8:35

Who can separate me from the love of God? Nothing and no-one.

Psalm 73:23

I am always with You Lord, You hold me by my right hand.

Matthew 28:20

You are definitely with me to the very end of the age.

Hebrews 7:25

I have drawn near to God and I am saved. Thank You Jesus, that You now always intercede for me, I am never forgotten.

FEELING UNAPPRECIATED AND UNDERVALUED

Romans 12:1

I offer my body as a living sacrifice, holy and pleasing to You Lord, this is my spiritual act of worship.

Romans 12:3

I do not think of myself more highly than I should but in accordance with the measure of faith I've been given.

Romans 12:11

I choose to remain zealous, to keep my spiritual fervour serving You Lord.

Romans 12:14

I choose to bless

I choose to live in harmony

I choose to live at peace with everyone

I choose to overcome evil with good

Romans 13:14

I cloth myself with You Jesus and refuse to think about how to gratify the desires of my sinful nature.

Romans 14:19

Today I will make every effort to do what leads to peace and mutual edification.

Romans 15:2

Today I choose to please my neighbour for his good, to build him up.

1 Corinthians 13:4

I am patient, I am kind, I will not envy, I will not boast, I am not proud, I am not rude, I am not self-seeking, I am not easily angered. I keep no record of wrong, I rejoice with the truth, I always protect, always trust, always hope, always persevere. I never fail!

Galatians 5:6

The only thing that counts today is my faith expressing itself through love.

Galatians 5:13

I choose to serve everyone else in love, to love my neighbour as myself.

Galatians 5:15-16

I refuse to keep on biting and devouring others, I will walk by the Spirit.

Ephesians 4:2

I choose to be completely humble and gentle

I choose to bear with others in love

I choose to make every effort to keep the unity of the Spirit through the bond of peace.

Galatians 6:7

I will serve wholeheartedly, as if serving You Lord, not men.

Isaiah 42:8 &10

Dearest Father, I repent of feeling sorry for myself. You alone are God, You alone deserve praise. I shift my focus back on you and sing You a song of praise and worship. I give You all the glory.

1 Timothy 4:12

I am not defined by how others see me. Rather I persist in setting an example for them in the way I handle myself; my speech, my love for others, my faith and my purity. I will not stop.

FEELING VULNERABLE

Matthew 10:16

I may feel like a sheep amongst wolves but You have given me the shrewdness and innocence to overcome today.

Matthew 10:19

I will not worry about what to say or how to say it today. The Spirit of my Father will speak through me.

Luke 12:22

I refuse to worry about my life, what I eat and what I wear.

Luke 21:31

I choose to seek first Your Kingdom today and know that You God, as my Provider will provide everything else.

John 14:1

I refuse to let my heart be trouble by …. My faith is in God my Father and the Lord Jesus Christ.

Hebrews 13:6

The Lord is my helper, I will not be afraid, man can do nothing to me.

1 Chronicles 22:13

I am strong and courageous, I refuse to fear or be discouraged.

Psalm 27:1

The Lord is my light, my salvation and my stronghold. I refuse to fear or be afraid.

Psalm 27:3

When an army attacks me I refuse to fear. When war breaks out against me, I will be confident.

Isaiah 43:5

I refuse to fear ..... God is with me.

Jeremiah 1:7-8

I refuse to say I am too young. I will go where You send me, I will say whatever You command me. I refuse to be afraid because You are with me and You will rescue me.

Jeremiah 51:46

I refuse to fear when I hear rumours.

Ezekiel 3:7-9

When people are hard-hearted and obstinate. I will not be a victim, I will not be afraid of them, I will stand my ground.

Luke 6:28-29

I pray a blessing on those who are mistreating me. I will not treat them as they are treating me, I will show them kindness.

2 Corinthians 12:9-10

Your grace is sufficient for me, Your power is made perfect in my weakness, when I am weak You show Yourself strong.

Isaiah 41:10

I will not fear or be dismayed because You are my God. You strengthen me, help me and uphold me in Your righteous right hand.

Revelation 12:11

I am more than enough for this situation, I am a conqueror through the blood of the lamb and the truth that I speak out.

FINDING MY VOICE

Proverbs 31:26

Father You are teaching me to speak with wisdom and to have faithful instruction on my tongue.

2 Corinthians 6:6

I speak with purity, understanding, patience and kindness in the Holy Spirit and in sincere love. I speak truth in the power of God - weapons of righteousness in both hands.

Ephesians 4:29

I will not let any unwholesome word proceed from my mouth but only such a word as is good for edification according to the need of the moment, so that it will give grace to those who hear.

Philippians 4:8

I choose to dwell on what is true, honourable, right, pure, lovely, good repute, excellent and praise worthy.

1 Thessalonians 4:18

I choose to use my words to comfort.

Hebrews 10:24

I choose to use my words to stimulate others to love and good deeds.

1 Corinthians 14:3

I will only prophesy to others, words that will bring them edification, exhortation and consolation.

James 1:19

I am quick to hear, slow to speak and slow to become angry.

2 Timothy 1:7

I do not have a spirit of timidity but I do have a spirit of power, love and discipline.

John 14:1

I will not let my heart be troubled, I believe in Jesus!

Proverbs 15:1

My gentle answer will turn away wrath, I refuse to speak harshly, it will only stir up anger.

Ephesians 4:25

I choose to put off falsehood and to speak truthfully to my neighbour.

Colossians 3:9

I will not lie to others, I have taken off my old self.

Matthew 12:34

I will speak out of the overflow of my heart, I will be careful what I speak.

Psalm 19:14

May the words of my mouth and the meditations of my heart be pleasing in Your sight O Lord, my rock and my redeemer.

Proverbs 15:28

I will not gush evil, I will weigh my answers.

Proverbs 21:23

I guard my mouth and tongue to keep myself out of trouble.

Ephesians 4:15

I have a choice to not just speak what's true about others which might be negative and judgemental but to speak the truth to them about who Jesus is in them and His good intentions for their lives.

Colossians 3:16

I fill my mind with the word of Christ today and allow all His richness to completely fill my heart. I use His wisdom to speak blessing, encouragement and advice to my brothers and sisters in Christ, permeating everything with thankfulness and gratitude.

FORGIVENESS

Colossians 3:12

I am chosen, I am holy, I am dearly loved so forgiveness is right. I choose to put on compassion, kindness, humility, gentleness and patience - so forgiveness is the only appropriate action.

Ephesians 4:31-32

I renounce all bitterness, rage and anger and I choose right now to be kind and compassionate to others. I forgive them just as in Christ I am forgiven.

Psalm 103:12

You have removed my sins as far as the East is from the West so I refuse to keep close another's sins against me.

Daniel 9:9

You Lord are merciful and forgiving to me even when I rebel against you. I choose to be like You and show mercy and forgiveness to people who don't deserve it.

Micah 7:19

You have trodden my sins underfoot and hurled my wickedness into the depths of the sea so I choose to follow Your example and forgive.

Matthew 6:14-15

I want to live in the good of Your forgiveness for me so I freely forgive others.

Matthew 7:3-5

I have been forgiven the 'plank in my eye' so I refuse to hold on to the 'speck in my brother's eye'.

Hebrews 10:17 and Jeremiah 31:34

You have chosen to forget my sins against You, You will not recall them. I choose to do the same, I will not keep a list or bring them up when provoked.

Mark 11:25

Father search my heart, is there anyone that I am holding anything against? I will not withhold forgiveness from them.

Colossians 3:13

I choose to bear with others and forgive the grievance I have. I choose to forgive because I am forgiven.

Matthew 18:35

I choose to forgive …. from my heart.

Matthew 18:22

I freely forgive …. again and I release them from the debt they owed me to ….

1 John 1:9

I will not withhold forgiveness from myself. I confess my sins right now …. and I declare that You are faithful and just to forgive me my sins AND cleanse me from all unrighteousness.

Luke 15:20-22

The moment my heart turns towards you in repentance You pour out Your compassion on me and I am held and loved. You restore me to my position of intimacy and authority, no recriminations ever.

Matthew 5:23-24

Father prompt me if I have anyone who has something against me. I will drop everything and as top priority I will first make sure we are reconciled in accordance with Your word.

GOD FIGHTS OUR BATTLES

Exodus 14:14

You fight for me, Lord I need only hold my peace.

Deuteronomy 20:3-4

I am bold, brave and confident, I refuse to give way to panic because You Lord go with me to fight against my enemies and give me the victory.

2 Chronicles 20:15

I am bold and confident because the battle is not mine, it's God's.

2 Chronicles 20:17

I take up my position of standing firm and I look to see the deliverance You will give me. I refuse to be afraid or discouraged. In boldness and confidence I go out to face.......... and You Lord will be with me.

Isaiah 41:10

I am fearless because you are with me, I am full of confidence because You are my God. You strengthen me and help me, You uphold me with Your right hand.

Psalm 34:17

Every single time I cry to You for help, You hear me and always deliver me out of all my troubles.

Psalm 18:39

You have equipped me for battle, You make those who rise against me, sink below me.

Psalm 118:6-7

You are with me so I'm bold, man can do nothing to me. You are with me, You're my helper, I will look in triumph on my enemies.

Ephesians 6:13

I put on the full armour of God to withstand evil and having done all, I stand firm.

Luke 10:19

I have Your authority to tread on serpents and scorpions and over all the power of the enemy, nothing will hurt me.

Isaiah 54:17

No weapon forged against me will prevail and I will refute every tongue that accuses me. This is my heritage and my vindication.

Isaiah 30:15

I return to You and rest in You and I'm saved. I am strengthened as I quiet my heart and trust You.

1 Philippians 1:28

I am not intimidated in any way by those who oppose me. This is a sign to them that they will be destroyed but that I will be saved - and that by God.

Isaiah 54:14

I am established on a foundation of righteousness. I am far from oppression because I refuse to fear. I am far from terror, it will certainly not come near me.

Isaiah 40:29

When I am weary You make me strong. When I am weak, You increases my power.

Deuteronomy 31:8

You, Lord go before me, You are with me, You will never leave me or forsake me. I refuse to be afraid or discouraged.

Joshua 1:9

I refuse to be afraid or discouraged. God is with me wherever I go. I am strong and courageous.

Psalm 27:1

I refuse to fear because God is my light and my salvation. I refuse to be afraid because the Lord is the stronghold of my life.

GOD MY HEALER

Exodus 23:25

We will continually worship You our God and Your blessing will be on our food and water. You will take away sickness from us.

Isaiah 53:5

You took our punishment onto Yourself Jesus and bought our peace. By Your wounds I am healed.

Jeremiah 30:17

You will give us back our health and heal our wounds.

Psalm 103:3

You forgive all our sins and heal all our diseases.

Jeremiah 33:6

You Lord bring me health and healing. You will heal me and let me enjoy abundant peace and security.

Exodus 15:26

You are the Lord who heals me.

Deuteronomy 7:15

You Lord keep me free from every disease.

Psalm 41:3

You Lord nurse me when I'm sick and restore me to health.

Proverbs 4:22

Your word is life to me and heals my flesh.

Matthew 4:23

Lord Jesus You healed every disease and sickness.

Matthew 10:1

I have Your authority to heal every disease and sickness.

Matthew 10:8

Regardless of my current health status, I will continue to pray for and heal the sick because freely I have received so freely I give.

Psalm 107:20

You Lord send forth Your word and heal me and rescue me from death.

Jeremiah 17:14

Lord heal me and I will be perfectly well, rescue me and I will be perfectly safe. You are the One I praise.

Psalm 30:2

Lord my God I call to You for help and You heal me.

Isaiah 41:9-10

I am Your chosen Lord and You are with me so I refuse to fear. I am not dismayed because You are my God. You strengthen and help me, You uphold me with Your righteous right hand.

James 5:14-15

I will receive prayer and anointing of oil from the elders of the church when I am sick and the prayer of faith will save me as You Lord raise me up. If it was connected to a sin I have committed I repent and receive Your forgiveness.

Isaiah 58:6-8

I choose to stand up for the oppressed and to be generous to the poor in every circumstance.

I thank You Lord that then Your blessings over my life will quickly appear including my healing.

GOOD EXPECTATIONS

Romans 8:25

I am hopeful for what I can't yet see and with perseverance I wait eagerly for it.

Proverbs 10:28

I am Your righteous and my expectations end in joy and gladness.

Psalm 5:3

Every morning I lay out the pieces of my life on Your altar and I wait expectantly for Your fire to descend.

Philippians 1:6

I am confident that You Lord who started a good work in me will carry it on to completion until the day of Christ Jesus.

Philippians 1:20

I have a firm hope and expectation that I will never be ashamed and I am filled with courage now as always, so Christ is exalted in my body whether by life or by death.

Proverbs 15:15

I reject despondency that expects trouble and I choose a cheerful heart that has a continual feast.

Isaiah 30:18

I am so blessed as I wait for You in full expectation that You are waiting to be kind to me and to show me compassion.

Lamentations 3:25

Father You are good to me always. My hope is in You as I seek You and wait patiently for You.

Romans 15:13

I trust in You my God of hope and You fill me to overflowing with joy, peace and hope in the Holy Spirit.

Lamentations 3:22

Your steadfast love for me Lord never ceases, Your mercies never end, they are new every morning, You are faithful to me.

Psalm 62:5

I silence the noise in my head and focus my thoughts on how rock solid my hope in God is.

2 Corinthians 9:8

Lord You know my needs and You say that You will GENEROUSLY provide all I need. I look for Your provision and expect to have more than enough so I can share the excess with others.

Proverbs 11:23

I am righteous in Christ and my righteous desires always turn out well.

Hebrews 4:16

I come before Your throne full of confidence in Your grace and fully expecting to receive mercy and grace to help me in time of need.

John 15:5

Lord Jesus You are the vine and I am a branch, as I wait patiently and rest in You, I will bear much fruit.

Psalm 146:5-6

I am so blessed because the creator of the universe is my helper and my hope is in Him.

GRATEFULNESS

1 Chronicles 16:8-12

I choose to thank You Lord and call on Your Name. I will make known what You have done. I choose to sing praise to You and I will tell of all Your wonderful acts. I choose to rejoice right now, I will look to You and Your strength, I will seek Your face and I will remember the wonders You have done.

Psalm 107:1-20

I give You thanks right now for Your unfailing love and Your wonderful deeds. I cried out to You and You delivered me, You have satisfied my thirst and filled me with good things. You have delivered me from darkness and the deepest gloom and broken away my chains. You have sent forth Your word and healed me.

Psalm 107:29-30

You still the storm to a whisper, You have hushed the waves of the sea, You have brought me calm and You guide me to my desired haven. I give You thanks right now for Your unfailing love and Your wonderful deeds.

1 Corinthians 15:57

I give You all the thanks because You have given me victory over sin and death through my Lord Jesus Christ.

1 Thessalonians 5:16-18

I choose joy right now, I choose to talk to You about everything, I choose to be thankful right now, this is Your will for me in Jesus.

Revelation 7:12

All praise and glory and wisdom and thanks and honour and powder and strength to You my God forever and ever.

Philippians 4:4-6

I choose to rejoice right now because You are near me. I renounce anxiety, I reject it and I choose to talk to You about my concerns and my requests - You are worthy right now.

Psalm 23

You are my Good Shepherd and I never lack anything. You give me lasting peace and always restore my soul. You give me a continual feast in the face of difficulties, my cup overflows. Thank You Father that Your goodness and mercy are always around me and heaven awaits me.

Psalm 100:1-5

I will shout with joy to You Lord and I will serve You today with gladness. I sing of Your goodness, I belong to You and Your steadfast love and faithfulness will never fail. I give You all the praise and thanksgiving and I bless Your Name.

Psalm 118:24

You have made this day Father no matter how it's looking right now. I choose to rejoice and be glad for it as I expect You to do good things.

2 Corinthians 2:14-16

I give You all the thanks Father that in Christ You always lead me in triumph and spread through me the aroma of Christ.

Philippians 4:12-13

I know how to be humble and I know how to prosper. In every situation I have learned the secret of contentment. I am empowered by Christ's strength within me to face anything.

Colossians 3:17

Every thought I have today and every action I choose to make, I will permeate with thankfulness to You my Father.

GUIDANCE

Isaiah 30:21

It doesn't matter whether I turn to the left or the right, my ears will hear Your voice behind me saying, "This is the way, walk in it."

Isaiah 58:11

The Lord will always guide me. He satisfies my needs when I am parched and He strengthens my frame. I am a well-watered garden, I am a spring who's waters never fail.

John 16:13

The Holy Spirit guides me into all truth. He will tell me what is yet to come.

Proverbs 11:14

Victory is mine as I seek guidance from many advisors.

Proverbs 16:9

I plan my course in my heart but You Lord establish my steps.

Proverbs 20:18

I will seek advice so my plans are established.

Psalm 32:8

I receive Your instruction and teaching on the way I should go. Thank You that You counsel and watch over me.

Psalm 32:10

My trust is in You Lord as Your unfailing love surrounds me.

Psalm 119:105

Your word is a lamp to my feet and a light to my path. Speak to me Lord from Your living word.

Psalm 37:23-24

I delight myself in You and You make my steps firm. I will not fall even if I stumble because You uphold me with Your right hand.

Proverbs 3:5-6

I submit my plans to You and I thank You that You will make my paths straight. I trust You with all my heart and I refuse to lean on my own understanding.

James 1:5-6

I ask You for wisdom and I receive Your wisdom right now by faith, believing that I have received it generously from You without any reserve.

Romans 8:28

You work all things together for good because I love You and I am called according to Your purpose.

2 Corinthians 5:7

I walk by faith, I refuse to make decisions based on just what my eyes can see.

John 15:7

I choose to abide in You Lord and I thank You that Your words abide in me. Based on Your word within me I ask You for whatever I wish and it will be done for me.

Psalm 25:12

I hold You in reverent awe at Your majesty and power and I thank You that You instruct me in the way I should choose.

Philippians 4:6-7

I refuse to be anxious, instead I pray and make my requests, giving You all the thanks of my heart. I receive Your peace and know that it will guard my heart and mind in Christ Jesus.

Psalm 37:7

I will be still before You Lord, I will wait patiently for You. I will not fret.

Proverbs 2:6

You give me wisdom, from Your mouth comes my knowledge and understanding.

I CAN'T DO IT!

Philippians 4:13

I can do all things through You, You strengthen me.

1 Corinthians 10:13

This trial I am facing is not unusual, it is being faced by many others too but I declare that God You are faithful and You will not allow me to be tempted beyond what I can bear and You WILL provide a way out for me.

2 Corinthians 12:9

I declare that Your grace is all I need and that Your power works best in my weakness so I will boast about my weaknesses so that it's not my own efforts that I rely on but the power of Christ working through me.

Isaiah 40:29

Thank You Father that You strengthen me when I'm weary and You increase my power when I am weak.

Proverbs 3:6

Lord I give this situation to You, I acknowledge Your sovereignty and declare that You will create a straight path through for me.

Ephesians 6:10

I am strong in the Lord and in His mighty power.

Matthew 19:26

Jesus You say, "With man this is impossible but with God all things are possible".

Luke 1:37

I declare over this situation that nothing is impossible for my God.

Matthew 17:20

I may only have a small amount of faith but I can still say to this 'mountain' move and it will move. Nothing will be impossible for me.

Mark 11:24

Lord Jesus, You said it so I believe it. Whatever I ask for in prayer, I have received it, it is mine.

Isaiah 41:10

I am not alone, You strengthen me and help me, You uphold me with Your righteous right hand.

Jeremiah 32:17

Lord You made the heavens and the earth by Your power and out stretched arm so nothing is too hard for you.

Romans 8:31

Nobody and nothing can be against me because God is with me.

Isaiah 40:31

I place my trust in You Lord and I find my strength renewed. I am able to rise above this situation like an eagle. I have the energy and the strength for this, I can keep going without failing.

Psalm 28:7

I trust You with all my heart Lord because You are my strength and my shield. I am full of joy and thanksgiving as I remember that You always help me.

Ephesians 3:16

I declare that out of God's glorious riches I am strengthened with the Holy Spirit's power in my innermost being.

I FEEL SO ANGRY BUT I DON'T WANT TO SIN!

Proverbs 14:29

I choose to control my anger by being understanding. I will not be foolish and display hot temper.

James 1:19

I am quick to hear, slow to speak and slow to anger.

Proverbs 15:1

I choose to answer softly because it turns away wrath in me. I will not speak harsh words as that stirs up anger in me.

Proverbs 18:2

I take pleasure in understanding and not just in expressing my opinion.

Ephesians 4:29

I will not let any foul or abusive language come out of my mouth. I choose to only speak what will build up and bring grace to the situation.

Ephesians 4:32

I am kind and tendered hearted. I choose to forgive him/her as God in Christ has forgiven me.

Proverbs 16:32

I am patient and I am in control of my spirit.

Proverbs 16:21

My sweetness of speech is more persuasive than anger.

Proverbs 10:19

Too much talk leads to sin. I choose to be sensible right now and keep my mouth shut.

Ephesians 4:26

When I feel angry, I will not sin. I will not let the sun go down on my anger.

Proverbs 18:13

I will always listen first, really listen, before I give my answer.

Luke 6:45

I will speak only good to him/her out of the abundance of my heart.

Proverbs 11:12

I will display understanding and I will not belittle him/her.

Titus 3:2

I will not say cruel things or argue. I am gentle and show perfect courtesy.

Colossians 3:12

I am God's chosen one, I am holy and dearly loved so I put on a compassionate heart, kindness, humility, meekness and patience.

Isaiah 30:15

In my quietness and trust shall be my strength.

Proverbs 14:30

I repent of jealousy that eats away like cancer and I embrace Your tranquility right now. I speak peace to my heart it is life to my body.

Proverbs 15:28

I will not gush evil, I will weigh my answers.

2 Timothy 1:7

I do not have a spirit of timidity but I do have a spirit of power, love and discipline.

LIVING IN FREEDOM

1 Corinthians 6:17

I am united with the Lord and I am one with Him in spirit.

Romans 6:6

My old self has been crucified with Christ, my body, ruled by sin has been done away with, I am no longer a slave to sin.

Galatians 5:22

I am increasingly fruitful in love, joy, peace, patience, kindness, goodness, faithfulness, gentleness and self-control.

1 Corinthians 13:4-7

I am patient, I am kind, I am not jealous, I do not brag, I am not arrogant, I do not act unbecomingly. Rather I bear all things, believe all things, hope all things, endure all things.

Galatians 5:1

It is for freedom that Christ has set me free. I will stand firm then and not let myself be burdened again by a yoke of slavery.

Ephesians 3:12

Father I can approach You with freedom and confidence through faith in Jesus.

Psalm 119:45

I have been released to walk about in freedom and to seek out Your ways.

Romans 6:22

I have been set free from sin. I walk into freedom in Jesus' name. I will think and act as a slave of God in holiness and eternal life.

1 Peter 2:16

I will live free and not use my freedom to cover up evil anymore.

Colossians 1:22

I have no blemish and I am free from accusation before God.

I choose to stay deeply rooted and firm in my faith and never move away from this hope in the gospel.

Romans 8:1-2

There is no condemnation over me, I am in Christ Jesus. The law of the Spirit of life has set me free from sin and death.

Isaiah 61:1

I have been released to be who God created me to be. I have been released from darkness, God has bound up my broken heart and I am now anointed and have a calling to pass on the good news and proclaim freedom and release to others.

Proverb 4:23 and 2 Corinthians 10:5

I guard my heart and I take every thought captive and make it obedient to Christ. Every argument and pretension in my head that is negative, self-serving, self-pitying or proud I capture and receive the opposite in power.

John 8:36

Jesus has set me free so I am totally free.

1 Corinthians 6:12

I am free to do whatever I want but not everything is good for me so I refuse to let anything control me.

Romans 6:14

Sin no longer rules over me because I live under the freedom of God's grace.

LOVING OTHERS

Romans 15:7

I choose to accept others just as Christ has accepted me in order to bring praise to God.

Romans 12:9

I am sincere, I refuse to just pretend to love others. I hate evil and I cling to what is good.

Romans 12:10

I am devoted to my brothers and sisters in God's Kingdom. I honour each one of them more than myself.

Romans 12:13

I am generous with my time, my possessions and my money.

I practice hospitality every week.

Romans 12:14

I pray good things over those who are nasty to me.

Romans 12:15

I choose to be happy with those who are happy and to mourn with those that mourn.

Romans 12:16

I choose to live in harmony with others. I refuse to be proud or conceited and I am happy to enjoy the company of the lowly.

Colossians 3:12

I am God's child, loved and chosen. So then I clothe myself with compassion, kindness, humility, gentleness and patience with love.

Colossians 3:13

I am tolerant of others.

I forgive every single time I have a complaint against another.

Micah 6:8

I am fair and just in my dealings. I will stand against injustice.

1 Thessalonians 5:15

When people are hateful to me I refuse to be hateful back. Instead I will always try to do what is good for them.

Luke 6:27-28

I choose to be kind and generous even when it hurts.

Romans 12:3

I refuse to elevate myself but I remind myself who God is and the mercy I have been shown.

1 John 4:18-19

I can be loving towards others because I am so loved.

I am not fearful to be loving. I reject fear, I root it out, I am free to love.

Timothy 1:5

I am called to love from a pure heart, a good conscience and a sincere faith.

James 3:18

I am a peacemaker - I sow in peace that I might reap a harvest of righteousness.

1 Peter 4:8

I will always love others deeply because love covers a multitude of sins.

James 2:1-12

I refuse to treat anybody differently depending on whether they have money or not and I refuse to show favouritism. I will treat everyone I meet with mercy.

James 2:14-17

If I see a need and I have the means to meet it, I will. I will show love with action not just words.

MY WORKPLACE

Ecclesiastes 10:4

If a ruler's temper rises against me, I will not abandon my position, my composure will allay great offences.

Colossians 3:23

I will work at whatever I do with all my heart as if I am working directly for You Lord.

Deuteronomy 15:10

I choose to give generously to the poor without a grudging heart then You will bless me in all my work and in everything I put my hand to.

Proverbs 14:23

All my hard work brings a profit, I refuse to waste my time with mere talk that brings poverty.

Psalm 90:17

Your favour is on me Lord and You establish the work of my hands.

Proverbs 12:11

I will work hard today and enjoy Your provision, I refuse to waste time chasing fantasies.

Philippians 4:13

Father I receive Your strength today to face anything that comes.

Colossians 3:24

My eyes are back on You O Lord, it is You only that I serve today and my reward is Your inheritance.

Proverbs 12:24

I will work hard today as I am called to be a leader who's in control. I refuse to give into laziness that only brings slavery.

Genesis 2:3

I commit to honour Your sabbath rest and I will take a rest from work every seven days.

Titus 2:7

I will always set an example for others. I will act with integrity and diligence.

Proverbs 13:4

I will not be led by my cravings that produce nothing but I will be diligent and be fully satisfied.

Philippians 2:14-15

I will work hard without grumbling and complaining so that my colleagues see my light.

Colossians 3:17

Everything I do and say today, I will do it all in the name of You Lord Jesus, giving thanks to my Father through You.

Ecclesiastes 9:10

Whatever my hands find to do today I will do it with all my might.

Proverbs 22:1

I choose a good name over wealth. I choose favour over silver and gold.

Luke 16:10

I choose to be trustworthy with the little things. I choose to be honest with the little things.

Genesis 39:23

O Lord be with me as You were with Joseph, cause everything I do to succeed.

Malachi 3:6

I choose to give the full tithe, to be generous and open-handed and I expect Your outpouring of blessing.

Proverbs 10:22

May I be rich through Your blessing Lord. Your riches have no sorrow attached.

Psalm 127:2

I refuse to stress through 'busyness'. You build my house while You grant me rest and sleep.

PEACE NOT ANXIETY

Psalm 119:76

Father Your unfailing love is my comfort.

John 14:27

I have Jesus' peace so I refuse to be troubled and I refuse to be afraid.

Jude 1:2

Mercy, peace and love are mine in abundance.

Psalm 31:21

Thank You Father that when I am surrounded and attacked You reveal Your amazing loving kindness to me.

Psalm 118:5

I cry out to You Lord when I am hard-pressed and You bring me to a spacious place.

1 Corinthians 3:16 and 2 Timothy 1:7

I have the Holy Spirit of God living inside me and He has not given me a spirit of fear. He has given me power, love and a sound mind.

Isaiah 35:4

I am strong and I will not fear because You have promised Father to rescue me and make everything right.

Isaiah 40:28-31

Lord I feel so weary and weak but You are full of strength. You're never tired or weary and You are poised ready to pour fresh strength into me as I step back and rest in You right now. I receive Your renewed power to rise above my problems and emotions and run with fresh vigour.

Isaiah 41:10

I reject fear and refuse to be dismayed because You are my God and You strengthen me and help me. I am held in Your righteous right hand.

Matthew 6:25-32

I refuse to entertain worry about the practicalities of my life like food and clothes. I choose to look again at nature and acknowledge afresh how faithful, rich and attentive You are my loving Heavenly Father. If You bother to care about sparrows and lilies then how much more are You committed to me!

Matthew 6:33-34

My focus today is fully on Your Kingdom and Your righteousness Lord.

Luke 12:12:32-34

I reject fear because I have been given the Kingdom. In the face of my financial worries I choose to be generous and give away to the poor. I am building up for myself treasure in heaven, that's where my heart is.

Psalm 34:4

I have asked You Lord for help and You have heard me, You have delivered me from all my fears. I will not take them back again.

Psalm 94:19

When doubts fill my mind, Your comfort gives me renewed hope and joy. I receive it!

Philippians 4:6-7

I refuse to be anxious and I choose to talk to You Lord right now about what I need with a heart full of thankfulness. I receive Your peace that promises to guard my heart and mind in Christ Jesus.

Matthew 11:28-30

Father this weight feels too much for me, I am weary and burdened. You promise me Your rest so I take up your easy yoke and light burden and leave my heavy weights for You to carry. Thank You Father.

Psalm 37:7-9

I will rest in You Lord and wait patiently for You. I will not fret, I will not get angry, I renounce wrath. I will wait for You Lord and inherit the land.

Colossians 3:15-17

I allow the peace of Christ to rule in my heart today as I remember my place in His body the church and resolve to live in peace with others. I am so thankful.

PRACTISING 'LONG-SUFFERING' WHEN ALL YOUR BUTTONS ARE PUSHED

Fill in the person's name in the blanks

Long-suffering means 'long of nose/breathing' i.e. slow to anger. It means great kindness and plenteous in mercy. It is associated with joy, a joyful acceptance of the will of God whatever it might be.

2 Timothy 1:7

I am not timid, the Holy Spirit gives me power, love and self-discipline.

Philippians 4:8

I turn my back right now on all the negative thoughts I'm having about .... and I choose to remember all their good qualities and all the times they've got it right - all that is true, noble, right, pure, admirable, excellent and praiseworthy.

Colossians 3:15

Right now, in the heat of this moment, I allow and invite the peace of Christ to rule in my heart because .... and I, as members of one body, are called to peace. I choose to be thankful for them right now.

James 1:19

I take a step back, I choose to stop talking and to really listen to what .... is saying. I refuse to give vent to my angry feelings because they cannot produce the righteousness that God desires. I humbly receive Your word of grace right now which saves me from my angry reactions.

1 Corinthians 9:26-27

I will not fight like a boxer, beating the air. Instead I take control of my body, my tongue and my emotions right now.

2 Peter 1:3-9

I declare that Your divine power has given me everything I need to be godly in this situation. I ask You for fresh faith, goodness, self-control, mutual affection and love. I choose to remember that I have been cleansed from all my past sins - they have no hold over my emotions now.

Ephesians 6:10-18

My struggle is not with .... the enemy is stirring me up with lies and negative emotions. I choose to take my stand right now, I take my eyes off .... and I put on the full armour of God - the helmet of salvation, the breastplate of righteousness, the belt of truth and the shoes of the readiness of the gospel. I raise up the shield of faith and I speak out the sword of the Spirit - God has victory for me in this situation, I can control my tongue and my emotions and I will stand my ground in peace and joy as an overcomer.

Galatians 5:13-26

I declare that I am free, the past has no hold on me. I am free to treat .... with love, kind words, restraint and long-suffering, to treat .... as I would like to be treated. I repent of discord, jealousy, rage, hatred and any other negative emotion. I have crucified my flesh and my hot emotions and I step into line with the Holy Spirit and embrace His peace and joy right now.

Titus 2:2+5+12

I am temperate, self-controlled and my faith, love and patience never fail. I am pure and kind and I put .... first. I say no to worldly passions and I say yes to self-control and godliness.

James 3:6+14

I repent that I have used my tongue to speak angrily/critically/judgementally/abusively/unkindly. I stop my talking and I examine my heart instead. Why am I reacting like this? Am I harbouring bitterness, unforgiveness or selfish ambition? I repent of those and I forgive everyone I have held a grudge against (list each individual). I choose to peacefully respond with consideration, submission, mercy, impartiality and sincerity.

James 3:18

I am a peacemaker. I will sow peace into this situation and I will reap a harvest of righteousness.

Printed in Great Britain
by Amazon

68914913R10045